MEMORIES
of the
MISAWA BAPTIST
MISSION

CLYDE C. WILTON
&
AARON Z. WILTON

Copyright © 2022 Clyde C. Wilton & Aaron Z. Wilton.

All rights reserved. No part of this book may be reproduced, stored, or transmitted by any means—whether auditory, graphic, mechanical, or electronic—without written permission of both publisher and author, except in the case of brief excerpts used in critical articles and reviews. Unauthorized reproduction of any part of this work is illegal and is punishable by law.

ISBN: 979-8-88640-052-6 (sc)
ISBN: 979-8-88640-053-3 (hc)
ISBN: 979-8-88640-054-0 (e)

Because of the dynamic nature of the Internet, any web addresses or links contained in this book may have changed since publication and may no longer be valid. The views expressed in this work are solely those of the author and do not necessarily reflect the views of the publisher, and the publisher hereby disclaims any responsibility for them.

One Galleria Blvd., Suite 1900, Metairie, LA 70001
1-888-421-2397

CONTENTS

Preface v

Chapter 1   Beginnings..1

Chapter 2   Misawa Baptist Mission 13

Chapter 3   Memorial Baptist Mission..31

Chapter 4   Misawa Baptist Church..49

Picture Credits 55

Index of Names 67

PREFACE

The recollections of the Misawa Baptist Mission in this work are primarily from Clyde Wilton while he served as a USAF Chaplain at Misawa AB, Japan, from July 1959 to June 1962, and the years that followed. While serving as a chaplain in Japan, Clyde was privileged to also follow a calling from the Lord to spread the Christian Gospel to the Japanese people. As an answer to the prayers of Clyde and a number of other military personnel, the Gospel message was implemented through the establishment of a Baptist Mission in the city of Misawa that came to be known as the Misawa Baptist Mission.

Long before there were any inklings of a Misawa mission, the Lord was working through Clyde Wilton even as far back as when he was born into humble beginnings on November 22, 1919. Clyde's early life was spent on a farm located 3 and 1/2 miles from the town of Jermyn, Texas. He was the youngest son of Elmer E. and Eula Wilton, and he had two brothers, Luther V. Wilton and Charles Anthony Wilton. About 1 and ½ miles to the east of the Wilton property was the community of Winn Hill, where the closest church, school, cemetery, and mail box were located. His world for about two decades consisted of acquaintances in farms nearby, the Kinnards and the Hubers, living about a mile over a hill to the north, and the Easters and the Crums, living about a mile east over Easter Hill.

During his early school years, Clyde first went to a one-room schoolhouse at Winn Hill, walking daily the three-mile round trip. After the school at Winn Hill consolidated with the Jermyn Public

School in 1931, he rode a bus to school each day to Jermyn until he graduated from high school in 1938.

After finishing high school, Clyde started college at Weatherford Jr. College in Weatherford, Texas. Then, in January 1939, he transferred to North Texas State Teachers College (NTSTC) in Denton, Texas. Clyde's religious training had begun while he was a member of the Bethany Baptist Church at Winn Hill, where he had made a commitment to the Lord at the age of thirteen; but, his first real encounter with eternal spiritual things was while he was at NTSTC. During his sophomore year, he began to struggle with the real meaning of life, pondering such notions as, "If this life is all there is, then all is in vain," and "What is the real purpose of education and achievement?" Up to that time while at college, he had become too busy to read his Bible, to pray, or to go to church. After his inner struggle, Clyde realized that the Lord was calling him to preach. He then surrendered to this call, and he preached his first sermon on March 3, 1940, at the Bethany Baptist church at Winn Hill, Texas. A short time later, in April 1940, Clyde left college and returned home to live for a while with his parents at the Wilton homeplace near Winn Hill, Texas.

The time spent at home away from school was about a year and a half. Once again there was time to pray, to read the Bible, and to go to church. After a time of reflection and re-commitment, Clyde returned to college in September 1941, this time going to a Christian institution, Howard Payne College, located in Brownwood, Texas.

Having no money, it was necessary to get a job while going to college. It was while being employed by the Puckett hamburger joint in Brownwood, Texas, that Japan bombed Pearl Harbor in Hawaii on December 7, 1941. At that time many young men were then drafted into military service, but because Clyde was in the gospel ministry, he was deferred from military service. By the time he graduated from college in 1943, the war was over.

It was while at Howard Payne College that Clyde met the love of his life, Larue V. Haley, who was also a Howard Payne student. They dated until Clyde graduated from college, and they were married on October 17, 1943, at the Bethany Baptist Church at Winn Hill, Texas. Larue was at his side throughout Clyde's ministry, and she was a major contributor to his success throughout the years that followed. For a time the couple served at a number of small Baptist churches in Texas. Then, in September 1945, Clyde continued his education at the Southwestern Baptist Theological Seminary in Fort Worth, Texas. After three years at the seminary, Clyde graduated with a Master's Degree, and in August 1948, he became the pastor of the 1st Baptist Church of Bellevue, Texas.

In 1949, while still serving as pastor of the 1st Baptist Church of Bellevue, Clyde petitioned the military for a commission as a chaplain in the USAF. He had first inquired several years earlier, but at that time he did not meet the age requirement. On this occasion his request was accepted, with his entry date into the USAF as a 1st Lieutenant to take effect on February 1, 1951.

After finishing military orientation at Brooks AFB in San Antonio, Texas, and then Chaplain's School at Carlisle Barracks, Carlisle, Pennsylvania, Clyde began his first military assignment at Chanute AFB, Illinois, located at Rantoul, Illinois. Following a year at Chanute AFB, he was assigned to Hickam AFB, Hawaii, beginning May 1952.

Beginning in December 1952, Clyde was transferred from Hickam AFB to Wheeler AB, where he completed his remaining service in Hawaii. Near the end of his time at Wheeler in February 1955, Clyde was granted educational leave for a tour through the East on "space available" status. It was during this educational tour that Clyde had his first encounter with Japan. On his tour, which went through Japan, Dhahran, Saigon, Bangkok, India, the Holy Land, and Hong Kong, one of the first stops was in Tokyo, Japan, on Sunday, February 13, 1955.

While in Tokyo, Japan, Clyde preached at the Haneda Chapel at the Tokyo International Airport. The title of his sermon was "I am not ashamed of the Gospel of Christ." There were military personnel at the service, and part of the message was to encourage them to take the opportunity to win the Japanese to Jesus. As was the custom in

Japan, many personnel had Japanese maids in their homes, which was an opportunity to share the Gospel. At the time there was no hint that Clyde might later also be among those serving in Japan.

After finishing the assignment in Hawaii, Clyde returned to the mainland, where he had duty assignments at Harlingen AFB in Harlingen, Texas, and Moore AB near Mission, Texas. After three years of duty in Texas, Clyde was then assigned to Misawa AB in Misawa, Japan. By that time, the Wilton family had grown to six members, with four children ranging in ages from 8 months to 13 years. Clyde had to leave the family behind in Texas until he could find a place for them to live at Misawa. Leaving them behind, even for the few months that it took, was one of the hardest things for him in making the change of address to Japan.

On Sunday, July 12, 1959, Clyde preached his first sermon at his new assignment at the Misawa AB Chapel. He quickly learned that there was a Baptist Worship Service that was held each Sunday afternoon at the Dependents High School building on the base. This was exciting news for him, and he attended the service on that day. One of the things that caught his attention after meeting SSgt. Calvin Doyle at the service was a wooden footlocker full of song books which were labelled, "The First Baptist Church." Wanting to possibly visit at this new place of service, he asked Calvin where the church was located. With a strange smile on his face, Calvin answered that the church did not yet exist, but by faith the Baptist Fellowship was planning and working for its establishment.

Clyde immediately recalled his first experience with Japan when he came briefly to Tokyo, Japan, in 1955. These were not the same people, but they shared the same gospel opportunities. On this day in July 1959, Clyde strongly felt a special calling to work with these dedicated Christians to make that new church a reality! As it turned out, that new church would not go by the name of the First Baptist Church, but it first came to be known as the Misawa Baptist Mission, later being named the Memorial Baptist Mission, and ultimately becoming the Misawa Baptist Church. For more than two years Clyde worked with the Baptist

Fellowship at Misawa until the Memorial Baptist Mission had its own building, which was dedicated on October 6, 1961. He continued to be a friend of the mission for the rest of his assignment in Misawa, Japan, and for many years after he returned to civilian life in Texas.

The work that follows consists of the history of the Misawa Baptist Mission and the memories of Clyde Wilton as he participated in this ministry with the Japanese people. Not only was he able to be a significant voice in the life of the church, but he made some lasting friendships with the members over the years. For some of those Japanese friends, he was able to sponsor preaching and education travels in the US; and, he was able to once again visit at the mission years later in 1991 for a final tour in Japan. The mission has been a lasting and important part of his outreach for Jesus Christ, and he is pleased to share his memories of this ministry.

CHAPTER 1

BEGINNINGS

Clyde Wilton was privileged to be present in Misawa, Japan, during the formative period of the Misawa Baptist Mission. His first connection with the mission was in 1959 when he was assigned as a USAF Chaplain at Misawa AB, Japan. He had been a Southern Baptist Chaplain with the USAF since 1951 and had served in posts at Illinois, Hawaii, and Texas, before coming to Japan in July 1959. Having never before heard of Misawa, Japan, it was one of the hardest things he remembered ever doing having to leave his wife and four children in Harlingen, Texas, to make the trip, even though they would be rejoining him months later.

Clyde Wilton

One of Clyde's first Japanese acquaintances was Junichi Ishikawa, who was the language specialist assigned to the Chapel at Misawa AB. Junichi meant in Japanese "Number One," but to those who knew him, he was called "Johnny." Johnny was a great help to all those associated with the chapel, but he was especially helpful to Clyde in finding housing so the Wilton family could make the trip to Japan. With Johnny's help, Clyde found a plot of land in B-Battery, located in Misawa City outside of Misawa AB. After buying the land, construction immediately began to build a new house. Although it was small by American standards, the house went up quickly, and the rest of the Wilton family made the trip to Japan in late August 1959, arriving in Misawa about September 10, 1959.

Wilton home at B-Battery in Misawa City, Japan, July 1959

Misawa is located in the northern region of the island of Honsu in the eastern Aomori Prefecture. The Misawa area, in the flatlands on the southern shore of Lake Ogawara and next to the Pacific Ocean, has been occupied by the Japanese since early times. American presence at Misawa Air Base began after WWII, and it is a joint operation with the Japan Air Self-Defense Force. Misawa currently serves as a combination industrial, commercial, and agricultural center, with Misawa AB making a large contribution to the local economy. Misawa City having a population of about 40,000 and Misawa AB a population of about 10,000, the nearest sizeable city is Hachinohe, which is 17 miles away. Tokyo, the nation's capital, is about 357 miles away to the south.

For as long as Americans have been present in Japan, there has been a tenuous relationship with the Japanese. Although they are very polite in public and they put value on personal accountability and working together, the Japanese are very private where the family is concerned. Largely due to the activity of some boisterous Americans from the base after dark, the American presence at Misawa AB did not have a good reputation among some Japanese. Being a Christian witness among the population there was hampered by this background and by the fact that the Japanese are largely dominated by Shinto and Buddhist religious beliefs. In Misawa City there were a few Christian churches at the time, but there was no Baptist church.

When Clyde arrived in Japan in July 1959, he preached his first sermon at his new place of service on July 12, 1959. It was on that same day that he learned that there was a group of airmen who were holding a Sunday Baptist worship service in the school building on the base. When he attended the service, Baptist hymnals were distributed from a wooden footlocker and marked in large, bold print, "The First Baptist Church." He was excited to hear about this possible place of service, but when he asked SSgt. Calvin Doyle about where it was located, Calvin just smiled and informed him that it was not there yet, but by faith there would be one there some day. That faith was eventually realized, but the church first came to be known as the "Misawa Baptist Mission" instead of "The First Baptist Church."

Calvin Doyle

Communicating with the Japanese people was a strange and wonderful adventure for Clyde. As long as he was on the military base, communication was not a problem. However, whenever leaving the safe confines of the base, it was sometimes a frustrating experience. As an example, shortly after arriving at Misawa, the family car, which had been sent earlier from the mainland, arrived at Hachinohe, Japan, a coastal city some 17 miles south of Misawa. The trip to the city was by a military bus in the company of other military personnel. The travel was a long, bumpy ride on a winding and dusty road that finally took them through the city and over a bridge to where the cars were located. Everyone was preoccupied with finding his own car and driving back to Misawa. By the time Clyde found his car and tried to get it started, the others were already driving up the hill and heading out of sight. At first his car started, but it then stalled out and would not go, leaving him stranded and alone. At that time, the sun was just a little above the western horizon and dropping fast. The thoughts that were in his mind brought memories of the recent bloody war with Japan, and he wondered how he might be received by the local people. There were no people around except the Japanese, and since he did not know how to speak their language, there was no way to communicate verbally with them. Since everyone had left him behind, he had no idea of how to get back to the base. It was a devastating feeling being half a world away from home alone in a strange land.

It was at that time of his deepest fears that help came along. Just before the sun dropped over the horizon, a military helicopter surfaced and landed nearby. In the helicopter was an Air Force pilot who had come to pick up his car. What a relief it was! For many years, it still thrilled Clyde to see in his mind that man coming toward his car and his good deed in providing a ride back to the base. Clyde did not remember the man's name, but he never forgot his kindness and help in that time of need. It was this experience and others that encouraged him to learn as much as possible about the Japanese language and customs.

The original push for a Baptist Mission in Misawa City came from an airman by the name of TSgt. Robert (Bob) Nickell. In 1958, after talking with many about this possible work, he received nothing but discouragement. Many so called "wise men" counseled that it was just not possible at that time. However, Bob Nickell was not looking for reasons why it could not be done, but he was seeking to find the way that it could be done. After praying and seeking the answer, there were finally others who were convinced that it could be done. On February 22, 1959, five Southern Baptist military personnel came together to organize a Baptist Fellowship, which was dedicated to the task of establishing a Baptist mission in Misawa City, Japan. Their names were: TSgt. Robert Nickell (Moderator), MSgt. George Ashcraft, MSgt. Richard Gates, SSgt. Franklin Jeffus (Corresponding Secretary), and SSgt. Kenneth Davis (Secretary). Due to military job rotation, some

Robert Nickell

of the original group left Misawa before the mission became a reality, but they prayed and worked and planted, and others came to continue their work.

In the lead-up toward establishing a Misawa Baptist Mission there were several things that first fell into place. The first activity of the Baptist Fellowship after its formation in February 1959 was to begin a regular Wednesday night prayer meeting, with the purpose of knowing the Lord's will concerning a Japanese mission and to generate interest in fellow Christians on the base. Then beginning on Easter Sunday, March 29, 1959, regular Sunday worship services were held, being led by different laymen. Also, the study courses, These Things We Believe and Soul Winning Doctrines, were completed by the group.

Beginning on May 6, 1959, SSgt. Alfred Martin became the interim pastor of the Baptist Fellowship. Also, a budget was adopted and trustees were elected to conduct business for the group, with MSgt. George Ashcraft as the chairman, and to inquire about the means to start the mission. For a while services were held at the Dependents School building at Misawa AB for English-speaking members, and services for the Japanese were held in Bro. Martin's home off the military base.

Alfred Martin *George Ashcraft*

On the advice of Southern Baptist Missionary, Edwin Dosier, members of the Baptist Fellowship began visiting Japanese Baptist

Convention churches in northern Japan. As a result, Pastor Tadashi Ohnuma from the Hachinohe Baptist Church agreed to assist the work in Misawa City. Beginning in June 1959, Ohnuma Sensei began coming each Thursday evening to conduct services in Bro. Martin's home for the Japanese. For the Sunday evening services with Bro. Martin, services were conducted with the help of a Japanese Christian by the name of Hiroshi Minokawa, who served as the interpreter.

Hiroshi Minokawa

At his new assignment at Misawa Air Base, Clyde Wilton was not alone in the desire to impact the Japanese people with the Christian gospel. Shortly before his arrival, there was another Southern Baptist Chaplain who came on staff at the base chapel, Chaplain Joseph Coggins. Beginning August 2, 1959, one of their first acts together was to move the Baptist Fellowship worship service for the English-speaking members from the base Dependents School building to the base chapel, where they became responsible for conducing services. It became a regular service of the chapel program that was first held on Sundays, but later in July 1960 it was changed to each Friday evening. It was an informal service and was attended by many who were not Baptists. For a long time the song leader was Airman Ronald Williams, a member of the Four Square Church, until he returned back to the mainland. After the mission was established, Ron also helped at the mission with the Japanese services. He was planning to enter the ministry, and with Clyde's assistance, Ron was able to get an early release from the military so he could go to the seminary in Los Angeles, California.

Joseph Coggins

Ronald Williams

As a member of the chapel staff, Junichi Ishikawa (Johnny) was a Japanese interpreter for all the chaplains at Misawa Air Base. He was probably one of the single most influential persons in helping to establish the Misawa Baptist Mission, and he became a very good friend. It was Clyde's privilege to baptize him and two other Japanese men on October 16, 1959, which, incidentally, was the same day as his wedding. Johnny was very zealous in his Christian faith, and he was instrumental in coordinating between the Christian military personnel and Japanese Christians. He was involved with organizing English classes for Japanese high school students, purchasing land for the Misawa mission, and helping to implement the entire mission project.

Junichi Ishikawa

In addition to the Baptist Fellowship, another organization concerned with communication with the Japanese people was the Voluntary Aid to the Needy Club (VAN Club), composed mainly of military personnel at Misawa AB. Many of the same people in the club were also members or associated with the Baptist Fellowship and the Baptist service at the base chapel. The VAN Club regularly scheduled field trips out into the Japanese community and provided yearly gift packages for the needy during the Christmas season. One of the first trips attended by Clyde Wilton was a trip to the Shingo/Herai Village near Aomori, Japan. In addition to helping members witness some of the Japanese culture, it was a time for fellowship with the membership. The trip included a train and bus ride into the countryside and a picnic lunch in the environs. For Clyde, it was also an opportunity to practice his checker-playing skills with friend John Andre.

VAN Club trip to Shingo/Herai Village, c. 3 Oct 1959

From Left: Clyde Wilton, Kathy Wilton, John Andre, c. 3 Oct 1959.

In the first week of September 1959, during the same time that the rest of the Wilton family was making the trip to Misawa, Japan, there was a revival held for the Japanese in Misawa City at the Misawa Jr. High School Gym. Two Japanese pastors conducted the revival with the help of other preachers and staff. Shortly after their first revival the Baptist Fellowship rented a building located across the street from the Junior High School in Misawa City. It was at that time that the former services held in the home of Bro. Martin were transferred to the newly rented building. The Missionary Donald Heiss from Aomori, Japan, who also participated in the revival, then began helping with the Thursday night services and a Bible class.

1st Misawa mission building

As a result of the witness among the Japanese, some of the first Japanese associated with the Baptist Fellowship services in Misawa City were Baptized on October 16, 1959. Johnny Ishikawa, along with Hiroshi Minokawa and Mamoru Yamagishi, were baptized in a local bathhouse by Clyde Wilton. At that time there were no other facilities available for a baptismal service, so the bathhouse was rented for the occasion and members of the fellowship attended to witness the event. These three converts in the mission work at Misawa were instrumental in helping to make the Misawa Baptist Mission become a reality.

Bathhouse baptism, Misawa City, Japan, 16 Oct 1959; From Left (squatting): Hiroshi Minokawa, Robert Nickell, Mamoru Yamagishi, Johnny Ishikawa.

Beginning about November 21, 1959, Clyde Wilton began teaching a Baptist doctrinal class in his home off the base at B-Battery, with Johnny serving as the translator for the Japanese. The classes were held on Saturdays for about three months at a time. As a result, there were a number of others who requested baptism. With there still being no baptismal facilities at the rented mission building, baptisms for new members were either conducted at local bath houses or in Lake Ogawara, located near Misawa AB.

*Wilton home at B-Battery, c. 21 Nov 1959;
From left: Hiroshi Minokawa, ___,
Clyde Wilton, Junichi Ishikawa, Tokichi Konno.*

In the continuing desire to start a Japanese mission in Misawa, Baptist military personnel met regularly in the home of MSgt. George Ashcraft to discuss possible plans to proceed. One of the big problems encountered was in getting a sponsor for the mission. After contacting several missionaries, pastors, and the leadership of the Japanese Baptist Convention, it was learned that the opinion of the Baptist leadership was that Misawa City was just not the right place for a new Baptist mission. The belief was that if the military base ever closed, the church probably would, too. This had happened before when an installation left, and it had been a great embarrassment to the Japanese Baptists. They were gracious and courteous, but they really did not want to be embarrassed by helping start a work that they thought was sure to fail. They came up with the idea that the fellowship might establish a Baptist work in another city that had a better location and more stable people to work with. However, the Baptist military personnel of the Baptist

Fellowship at Misawa were not discouraged by all the negative response of the Baptist leadership. They tenaciously believed that the Lord wanted them to establish a work in Misawa.

Still needing a sponsor, many trips were made to other churches in other cities. At one such visit to the dedication service for the Aomori Baptist Church at Aomori, Japan, on December 14, 1959, Clyde Wilton and Calvin Doyle conferred with missionaries Coleman Clarke and Don Heiss. It was at that time that a recommendation was made by Coleman Clarke that the Baptist Fellowship might seek sponsorship for the mission from the English-speaking Tokyo Baptist Church. In the follow-up that resulted, George Ashcraft and Calvin Doyle met with Milton DuPriest, the pastor of the Tokyo Baptist Church. The matter was then brought before the membership of the Tokyo Baptist Church, and on January 21, 1960, the church voted to accept the mission with its 29 charter members.

Milton DuPriest

CHAPTER 2

MISAWA BAPTIST MISSION

Shortly after the mission was accepted by the Tokyo Baptist Church, the fellowship was organized into several committees, with the moderator for the mission being George Ashcraft, and the clerk being Calvin Doyle. The committees were a Program Committee, consisting of Clyde Wilton, Joseph Coggins, and Alfred Martin, a Mission Committee consisting of MSgt. James Kelley, and a Finance Committee, consisting of Franklin Skaggs and Hiroshi Minokawa. Committee meetings were conducted on the second Monday of each month, and the monthly business meeting was on the third Wednesday evening of each month. The election for committee members was conducted once a year.

Misawa Baptist Mission building on B-Battery Road

Spurred on by successfully becoming a mission of the Tokyo Baptist Church, the fellowship sought to move into a slightly larger facility.

They soon found and leased a building on B-Battery Road in Misawa City. After making necessary alterations to convert the building into a suitable place of worship, the building was dedicated on February 3, 1960. The dedication message was given by Chaplain Joseph Coggins, and Clyde Wilton took part in the service, with Junichi Ishikawa serving as the English/Japanese translator.

*Dedication Ceremony, 3 Feb 1960;
From left (standing): Joseph Coggins,
Junichi Ishikawa, Frank Skaggs.*

The first business meeting in the new building was conducted on February 24, 1960. On Sundays there were two worship services, one at 11 AM and one at 7 PM. The doctrinal study class continued on Wednesday evenings, as necessary.

Also, about that time, there was a weekly English class started by Clyde Wilton and with the help of Johnny Ishikawa, who served as the translator. This class came as a result of a group of mostly Japanese high school students who wanted to learn English. The class had a twofold purpose, since it was the desire of the mission to share with them the gospel. To this end the Gospel of Matthew was used as the text for English classes. Over the time that Clyde was at

Clyde Wilton teaching

Misawa there were a number of Japanese who went through the class and became Christians and members of the mission. Clyde's opinion was that this class became the core of the Baptist work in Misawa City. Another valuable helper with this group was Airman Ronald Williams, who had a great ability to relate to the young people in addition to singing. Ron was also the music leader for the Baptist Worship Service at the Misawa Base Chapel.

After the formation of the Program Committee, a number of Japanese pastors and missionaries were invited to conduct services at the mission. Among those responding were Missionaries Don Heiss from Aomori, Carl Halverson of the Jordan Press, and Miss Hannah Barlow from Hakodate. As a further outreach, Don Heiss also conducted a Leadership Class for the Japanese laymen. Miss Barlow began coming from Hakodate on the island of Hokkaido to the mission each month for several days to conduct worship services and to direct and coordinate activities of the mission.

From Left: Carl Halverson, Mrs. Halverson, Mrs. Joyce Heiss, Donald Heiss.

Hannah Barlow

The Mission Committee, led by MSgt. James Kelley, was also active in efforts to communicate with other Japanese in the area. They visited with a number of Japanese Baptist churches to learn more about the programs and facilities of the churches in Japan. Among the first visited was the First Baptist

James Kelley

Church of Morioka, Japan, on February 21, 1960. This was a new church that was having meetings in the parsonage and had just started as a church in September 1959. The Baptist Fellowship was able to help with an offering and other support, and several follow-up visits were later made to Morioka. After a building program, the Morioka Baptist Church dedicated new church facilities on December 10, 1960. Also active with the Mission Committee were TSgt. Edwin Bateman and Miyoko Asano, who sometimes served as an interpreter. Another trip that helped to form relationships between the Japanese churches and the Baptist Fellowship at Misawa was to the Akita Baptist Church in March 1960.

Akita Baptist Church

On April 2-3, 1960, Toyohara Sensei from the Aomori Baptist Church made a visit to the Baptist Fellowship at Misawa. He and his wife also visited at the home of Clyde Wilton at Misawa AB. As of February 3, 1960, Clyde and family had moved from off the base to a residence at E-19 on the military base.

On May 14, 1960, Missionary Hannah Barlow visited with members of the Baptist Fellowship and the Misawa Baptist Mission at the home of Clyde Wilton. On the following day, Miss Barlow spoke at the Baptist Worship Service at the Misawa AB Chapel. This visit was an opportunity for fellowship and for Miss Barlow to share about her mission work in Hakodate on the island of Hokkaido.

Toyoharas

From Left: Hannah Barlow, Clyde Wilton.

Beginning about June 1960, communication was begun with Baptist Missionary Thomasine Allen of Kuji, Japan. Kuji was located in the Iwate Prefecture on the Japanese coast just 53 miles south of Misawa. She had been in Japan since 1915 and was in charge of the Kuji Christian Center, which included an agricultural school, a junior high school, a clinic, and a hospital. Miss Allen was well-spoken of by the Japanese and her students, and she had even received an Order of the Sacred Treasures from the Japanese emperor. After Clyde Wilton went to the Kuji center on June 28, 1960, Miss Allen visited with the Baptist Fellowship and the Misawa Baptist Mission on August 5, 1960. She made another trip to Misawa in February 1962, and she was an encouragement for the Baptist mission work.

Thomasine Allen

On July 22, 1960, a three-day revival was conducted at the Misawa Baptist Mission, led by Pastor Masaaki Amano from the Akita Baptist Church. Communication had begun with Amano Sensei as early as March 1960 when the Mission Committee with MSgt. Kelley made a mission visit to Akita. On Saturday, July 23, during the revival there was a picnic at Lake Ogawara sponsored by the VAN Club. At the event there were about 100 Japanese present and about 30 Americans, with Amano Sensei presenting a short message in Japanese; and two women from the mission were baptized by Clyde Wilton. Bro. Amano was a friend of the mission and communicated with Clyde for a number of years following the revival. In addition, Clyde was invited to preach at the Akita Baptist Church on October 23, 1960, with Miyoko Asano interpreting into Japanese.

*Misawa Baptist Mission revival,
c. 22 July 1960*

*Lake Ogawara, From left:
Masaaki Amano, Tokichi Konno,
Mamoru Yamagishi, (Ohnuma Sensei).*

Lake Ogawara picnic

During the year following the establishment of Misawa Baptist Mission, there were a number of new members added to the fellowship by baptism as a result of the ministry. New members, some baptized at a local bathhouse and some baptized at Lake Ogawara: Alfred Ronald Martin and Tokichi Konno on March 7, 1960; Taheshi Konno and Miyoko Asano on April 23, 1960; Fumiko Jones on May 30, 1960; Taeko Tonosaki and Kimie Straus on July 23, 1960; Marshall Madison on August 26, 1960; and Kenichi Yoshida on October 29, 1960. In addition, eleven Americans joined the mission by letter, making a membership of about forty-one. The Japanese members were encouraged to assume positions of leadership in the mission, since the American members eventually would be returning home to the mainland. In the following year, Japanese members, Junichi Ishikawa and Tokichi Konno were on the Program Committee, Hiroshi Minokawa was on the Finance Committee, and Miyoko Asano was the church clerk.

MISAWA BAPTIST MISSION

Kenichi Yoshida baptism at Lake Ogawara, 29 Oct 1960

In October 1960, the Misawa Baptist Mission was fortunate to have a distinguished visitor from the mainland by the name of Dr. James Wesberry. He came from the Morningside Baptist Church located in Atlanta, Georgia, and he was a great encouragement in the work of the mission. Dr. Wesberry had come to conduct a Protestant Preaching Mission at the Misawa AB Chapel on October 15, 1960 thru October 20, 1960. He was introduced to members of the mission and after meeting with them, he provided many positive things to say about the ministry of the mission.

Dr. James Wesberry

About February 1, 1961, Airman Bob Keith left Misawa to return to the mainland for another military assignment. Bob was the pianist for the Baptist Worship Service at the base chapel, and he had served with the fellowship Baptist service since it began in 1959. His last service at the base chapel was on January 27, 1961, and his valuable service in the music program and

From Left: Jean Coggins, Bob Keith, c. 1 Feb 1961.

other activities with the base chapel were missed. For several months afterward, Mrs. Larue Wilton served as the pianist in place of Bob until the arrival of SSgt. Willie Barefield.

In early 1961, about a year from the time that it was accepted by the Tokyo Baptist Church, the Misawa Baptist Mission decided that it should have its own building and property. This task was taken by the Mission Committee, with James Kelley as the chairman and Earl Varner as the Mission Moderator. In February 1961, Milton DuPriest, pastor of the Tokyo Baptist Church, came for a visit with the mission, and a financial goal of $8,000 was set for a building program. It was through the Baptist military personnel associated with the mission that a plan was formulated to raise the necessary funds. Since there was no outlet for securing a loan, many of the group pledged and paid a year's tithe in advance to help pay for the project. It was then possible to buy land and to erect a building, but there were also many hours involved with negotiations in the process. Johnny Ishikawa was the key player in these efforts, and it would not have been humanly possible without his help. He knew both the Japanese and English well, and because of his love for the Lord, he had a desire to see God's work accomplished. Johnny worked with the architect and the contractors from start to finish.

From Left: James Kelley, Earl Varner.

Milton DuPriest was also involved in the decision about where to purchase land for the mission project. A number of plots were examined and discussed after an extended search was made of the available land.

In April 1961, additional help was given by Coleman Clarke, Associate Secretary for Evangelism for the Japanese Baptist Convention, and Takeshi Fukuhara, a Japanese Baptist Deacon who was an expert in Japanese legal matters.

From Left: Earl Varner, Coleman Clarke, James Kelley, Takeshi Fukuhara.

After the land for the mission was secured, the Mission Committee had many meetings to discuss plans for the new building. When a plan was finalized about May 1961, an estimate of the building cost was presented to three contractors, and the construction project was granted to the Aiba Construction Co. Final negotiations for the building project were about July 10, 1961, with Mission member Tokichi Konno serving as Building Coordinator and TSgt. Thomas Chevallier as the mission treasurer.

From Left: Earl Varner, Tom Chevallier, __, Paul Hedler, __, Tokichi Konno.

On April 21, 1961, there was a special program for both Japanese and Americans that was presented at the Misawa AB Baptist Friday Service. A message was presented by Mamoru Yamagishi, with Missionary Hannah Barlow from Hakodate interpreting. In addition students from the Misawa City High School sang a special number in English at the service, and the American members sang the song, "What A Friend We Have In Jesus," in Japanese.

Misawa AB Chapel, 21 Apr 1961

On the following day, there was a baptismal service at a local bathhouse with Miss Barlow present and Clyde Wilton performing the baptisms. The Kawashima twins, Mutsu and Saki, were baptized, and they became faithful members of the mission.

Hannah Barlow (far left); Kneeling: Saki & Mutsu Kawashima.

From Left: Clyde Wilton, Mutusu Kawashima, Saki Kawashima.

With land negotiations completed for the new building and before construction began, there was a Groundbreaking Ceremony on June 4, 1961. For the occasion, a wooden cross was constructed and carried by both Japanese and American members from the meeting place on B-Battery Road to the building site for the new building. Japanese and Americans met together for the service, and afterward everyone enjoyed fellowship and a covered dish luncheon. Chaplain Joseph Coggins broke the ground during the ceremony, and Chaplain Clyde Wilton brought the groundbreaking message, with Johnny Ishikawa serving as the interpreter. There was also a choir group from the mission with Ronald Williams serving as the director.

Misawa Baptist Mission Groundbreaking Ceremony, 4 June 1961

Japanese members at the Groundbreaking Ceremony, 4 June 1961

It was shortly after the Groundbreaking Ceremony, about June 12, 1961, that Chaplain Joseph Coggins left Misawa. He was present at his last meeting of the Baptist Worship Service at the base chapel on June 9, 1961, and he was honored with a farewell banquet about June 10, 1961. That left Clyde Wilton as the only Southern Baptist Chaplain on staff at the Misawa AB Chapel. Clyde Wilton and his family then moved into the same quarters on the base that had been occupied by the Coggins family.

Joseph Coggins at Farewell Banquet, c. 10 Jun 1961

Beginning on June 19, 1961, the Wilton family went to the Family Inspiration Week that was held yearly at the Amagi Baptist Assembly at Amagi, Japan. Amagi was located on the Izu Peninsula south of Tokyo, Japan, and this was a religious retreat attended by many of the families of the Baptist Fellowship at Misawa. It was a time for reflection, fellowship, and relaxation, lasting for about a week until June 24, 1961. Missionaries Coleman Clarke and Donald Heiss, who were known to the Misawa group, participated in some of the program activities.

Amagi Assembly, 20 June 1961

Construction for the new mission building began in mid-July 1961. It was decided that the name for the mission would be changed from the Misawa Baptist Mission to the Memorial Baptist Mission. With construction lasting about three months, the dedication service for the new Memorial Baptist Mission was scheduled for October 6, 1961.

About the time in July 1961 that construction began on the Misawa mission building, another key person in the life of the mission arrived on the scene. His name was Hiroshi Suzuki, a Japanese college student who was then not a Christian but wanted to come to Misawa AB with the hope of learning more English. Hiroshi had been listening to the "Voice of American" program on the radio and he wrote a letter to the commanding General at Misawa AB requesting an opportunity to live with an American family for the summer. That request was passed from the General through the Chaplain in Charge at the Base Chapel, and eventually it came to Chaplain Clyde Wilton. After discussing it with his wife, Clyde invited Hiroshi to be a part of the Wilton family for the summer. For Hiroshi this was an opportunity to see firsthand how a typical American family with four children lived. On the other hand, for Clyde it was an opportunity to share with this Japanese young man the gospel of Jesus. When Hiroshi heard that his request was to be filled by a chaplain, he almost backed out of the deal. Hiroshi lived with the Wilton family from June 30, 1961 to September 11, 1961.

Hiroshi Suzuki

Hiroshi had the nickname of "Hero," which the Wilton family used with his approval, and his visit was the beginning of a wonderful relationship. Hero had the usual good manners and Japanese politeness. He taught the family many things about Japan, and he was delighted to do anything that was needed for him to do. For example, he was introduced to drinking buttermilk by Clyde Wilton, who liked buttermilk and usually had some in the house to drink. In what became to be known as the "buttermilk incident," when it was offered to him, Hero accepted it to be polite, not giving a hint about how he really felt. Later, when he learned that it was acceptable to be honest about his true feelings and that it was not necessary for him to drink the buttermilk, he was greatly relieved.

Since Hero was interested in learning more English, and Clyde was

From Left: Clyde Wilton, Hiroshi Suzuki.

interested in introducing him to Jesus, Hero was given the task of translating the Book of Matthew into Japanese. At that time Clyde was teaching the Book of Matthew to a group of young Japanese, with Johnny Ishikawa helping with translating, and there was the need for a text of the scripture in Japanese. Hero did a great job of translating the text from English into Japanese, and there was a time of great fellowship. Hero was also ready to teach Japanese to anyone who was interested in learning to speak Japanese, and for a while he even had an opportunity to teach Japanese to the base chapel staff.

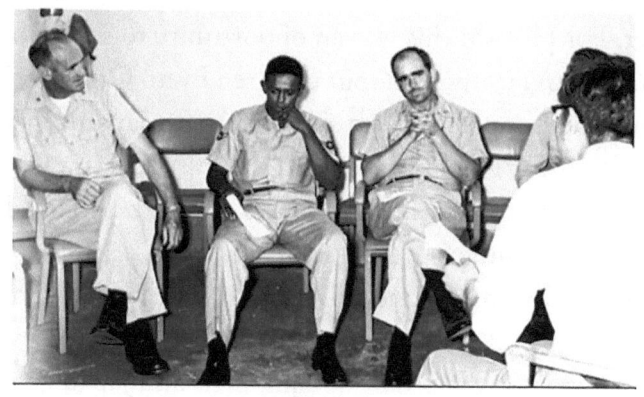

*Hiroshi Suzuki with
Misawa AB Chapel staff*

When Hero left Misawa in September 1961, he went back to his college studies, but he returned to Misawa in April 1963, becoming a Christian during a Misawa New Life Movement Crusade on April 20, 1963, and helping for a time with the mission work. Later, in 1967 Hero studied in the U.S.A. at Howard Payne College toward a M.A. Degree in English under the sponsorship of Clyde, and he began study at the Golden Gate Baptist Theological Seminary in Mill Valley, California, in 1970. Beginning in 1973, Hero had a job with the Southern Baptist Convention in New York, working with the Japanese people there. Eventually, he became a Christian counselor in New York.

Ronald Williams, another valuable workman in the early life of the Misawa Baptist Mission, left Misawa in August 1961 about the same time that Hero left after his summer at Misawa. Ron was the song leader at the Baptist Worship Service at the base chapel beginning about April 1960, and he had a gift of communicating with the young people at the mission. Ron was given a Sayonara party at the Wilton home about August 19, 1961. After returning to the mainland, Ron later served for twenty years as a missionary in Hong Kong and then as a teacher in a Bible college in Los Angeles, California.

Ron Williams (center) at Sayonara Party, c. 19 Aug 1961

Beginning in July 1961 and as the construction was progressing on the new building, members patiently watched in anticipation. First in place were the batter boards. The foundation was then begun and it was in place about July 22, 1961. Next, the walls were beginning to go up by July 27, 1961. Before the roof was in place, work began on the baptistery about August 7, 1961, and it was taking shape about August 10, 1961. The roofing began in earnest about August 12, 1961, and it was well on the way to completion by the time that the rear steps were progressing about August 18, 1961. The steeple and internal and exterior facing work began about August 23, 1961, and most of the work was done by September 30, 1961. The Misawa Baptist Mission sign that was at the old meeting place on B-Battery Road was removed about September 29, 1961.

Memorial Baptist Mission foundation construction, Misawa, Japan

Memorial Baptist Mission, Japan, Baptistery construction, c. 10 Aug 1961

Memorial Baptist Mission, Japan, Steeple construction, c. 23 Aug 1961

Sign removal at Misawa Baptist Mission site, c. 29 Sept 1961

Memorial Baptist Mission, Japan, c. 29 Sept 1961

About September 16, 1961, during the time that the mission construction was nearing completion, the Baptist Fellowship made a mission trip to a leper colony near Aomori, Japan. It turned out to be a surprisingly positive experience. Even though some of the lepers were visibly scarred by their disease, those who were members of the church at the colony had a joyful and gracious attitude. The Baptist Fellowship met with the colony for a time of sharing with Johnny Ishikawa serving as the Japanese interpreter. Even though they were not close enough to make physical contact, they were all in the same room for a time where some of the lepers gave their testimonies, and there was a great mutual Christian spirit that filled the room. It turned out to be a great day which Clyde would never forget.

Leper Colony, c. 16 Sept 1961

CHAPTER 3

MEMORIAL BAPTIST MISSION

As scheduled, the long-anticipated dedication service for the new Memorial Baptist Mission was held on October 6, 1961. Both American and Japanese members participated in the dedication service. Tokichi Konno gave the Call To Worship & the Scripture Reading; Junichi Ishikawa and Augustus Ramsey brought The Report; Earl Varner gave the Invocation; there was Special Music by Willie Barefield and the mission choir, which was directed by Larry Childers; Milton DuPriest brought the Dedication Message and Clyde Wilton gave the Dedication Prayer. Others who took part in the worship service were Taeko Tonosaki, Woodie Rhodes, James Kelley, and Alfred Martin. At the time of the dedication, there were twelve Japanese members of the mission, and they were taking the leadership, conducting the worship services and much of the administrative planning of the mission.

Tokichi Konno (left)

From Left: Junichi Ishikawa, Milton DuPriest.   *Augustus Ramsey*   *Clyde Wilton*

Memorial Baptist Mission Dedication Service, 6 Oct 1961

Shortly after the dedication of the mission, two of the military families involved in the life of the mission left Misawa for new assignments. The first to go were the Borrors, who left on October 16, 1961. Then, on November 20, 1961, Earl Varner, who was active as the Mission Moderator through the construction process, left Misawa for the mainland. Just a week later on November 28, 1961, the rest of the Varner family left to join him. The Varners, a family of six, and the Borrors, and their dedication to the Baptist Fellowship, were missed after their departure.

MEMORIAL BAPTIST MISSION

Borror Family

Varner Family

On November 29, 1961, the baptistery of the mission was put into use when there were multiple baptisms. Clyde Wilton performed the baptisms, which included two of his daughters along with four others. There was no longer a need to rent a bathhouse or go to the lake, since there was then an in-house baptistery.

Fawncyne Wilton baptism, 29 Nov 1961

Memorial Baptist Mission baptismal group, 29 Nov 1961

As was the normal practice each year, the VAN Club (Voluntary Aid to the Needy Club), prepared Christmas packages, but this year they took part in the Christmas program at the Memorial Baptist Mission. The Christmas program for Japanese children at the mission was on December 24, 1961. There were 94 present, and some of the Christmas packages prepared by the VAN Club were presented to the children. In addition to its Christmas work, the VAN Club was involved in helping provide assistance in a variety of ways to many of the churches of Northern Japan, and they had a program of visiting in area hospitals.

About the time of the Christmas program in 1961, the Sandbergs, another of the families working with the Baptist Fellowship, left Misawa. Bonnie Sandberg was involved in the Japanese Bible Class of the mission, and she was a leader in VAN Club. It was after helping with the yearly preparations of the Christmas packages that the family left Misawa.

Bonnie Sandberg during VAN Club preparations (standing right), c. 16 Dec 1961

Sandberg Family

On January 12, 1962, the Japanese Young People from the Aomori Baptist Church, accompanied by their pastor, Ken Hotai, participated in the Friday evening Baptist Worship Service at the Misawa AB Chapel. The speaker for the service was Missionary Don Heiss, also from Aomori, and a special offering was collected for the Aomori Baptist Church. The young people spent that night in Baptist Fellowship homes and returned to Aomori the following day.

From Right: Don Heiss, Ken Hotai, Aomori Baptist Church Young People.

MEMORIAL BAPTIST MISSION

As of January 14, 1962, a donation of 252,000 Yen ($700 dollars at that time) was received by the Memorial Baptist Mission on behalf of the Tokyo Baptist Church to help pay off remaining debt on the construction of the new mission building. The payment was in the form of a bank draft as a loan through the Southern Baptist Convention Foreign Mission Board to the Tokyo Baptist Church. The repayment of the loan by the Tokyo Baptist Church constituted a contribution to the building fund of the Memorial Baptist Mission.

Another special guest, Missionary Thomasine Allen, visited the Baptist Worship Service on February 9, 1962. She was accompanied by Takeshi Yahabe, both from Kuji, Japan, who had been working with Miss Allen for many years. Bro. Yahabe brought the message for the service, while Miss Allen translated from the Japanese. A Special Offering was also collected for the Kuji Christian Center.

From Left: Takeshi Yahabe, Thomasine Allen.

Beginning on February 15, 1962, a two-day Pastor's Evangelistic Conference was hosted at the Memorial Baptist Mission. Milton DuPriest from the Tokyo Baptist Church directed the conference, and there were in attendance about 8 Japanese pastors and several missionaries.

Evangelism Conference at Memorial Baptist Mission, 15-16 Feb 1962

On April 6, 1962, Shimizu Sensei from the Kytoto Baptist Church spoke at the Misawa AB Baptist Worship Service. On the following day, there was a fellowship meal at the home of Clyde Wilton at Misawa AB.

Shimizu Sensei

Shimizu Sensei (right) at fellowship

The first Easter service at the Memorial Baptist Mission was held on April 22, 1962. On this day there was an Easter Sunrise Service at 6 AM followed by a baptismal service. Three new members, Betty Jo Adams, L.C. Johnson, and John Meade were baptized, and members gathered for pictures after the service at the new building.

Easter Sunday, 22 Apr 1962   *New Members, Easter Sunday, 22 Apr 1962*

As June 1962 approached, the time for the Wilton family to leave Misawa drew near. On June 9, 1962, there was a Sayonara party for the Wiltons at Lake Ogawara, and about the same time there was a farewell meeting at the Memorial Baptist Mission. Then, on June 25,

1962, the final farewells were given as the Wiltons boarded the plane at Misawa AB for the trip back to the mainland. After the family spent a couple of days in the Tokyo area, Clyde Wilton preached a sermon at the Wednesday evening service at the Tokyo Baptist Church, and then on June 29, 1962, the family left Tachikawa AB on a flight to Travis AFB in California. On arrival in California, Clyde Wilton left military service to seek placement as a civilian Baptist preacher.

Sayonara Party for Clyde & Larue Wilton at the Memorial Baptist Mission, Misawa City, Japan, c. 9 Jun 1962

Beginning about October 1962, the choir at the Memorial Baptist Mission became known publically in the Christian community for its music under the organization and promotion by Junichi Ishikawa. The musical group was named the FHC Choir (Faith, Hope, Charity Choir). One of its first activities was to participate in the Misawa Musical Crusade held on October 25, 1962, at the Yurakuza Theatre in Misawa.

On December 23, 1962, the Memorial Baptist Mission had its second Christmas program since moving into its new building in October 1961. By then the membership had grown and there was a regular choir with new choir robes. As was the original goal by the Baptist Fellowship, the Japanese membership became more in charge of the worship and administration of the mission.

On March 22, 1963, there was a special ordination service at the Memorial Baptist Mission. Member Thomas Chevallier was ordained as a deacon. The service was presided over by Milton DuPriest, and several deacons and the assistant pastor of the Tokyo Baptist Church attended. At the service the Lord's Supper was observed and there was one baptism.

Tom Chevallier

In his capacity as a Japanese translator, Junichi Ishikawa was privileged to work with New York Metropolitan Opera soloist, Irene Jordan, when she came to Japan on a singing tour. About March 30, 1963, Miss Jordan appeared for a recital at the Aomori City Auditorium as part of the New Life Movement in Japan. After her performance, she gave her Christian testimony to an audience of over 12,000 with Junichi Ishikawa serving as an interpreter. Through his participation with Miss Jordan, one of the newspapers promised to publicize the upcoming New Life Texas Crusade planned for Misawa in April 14-20, 1963.

In the continuing support of the New Life Movement, Junichi Ishikawa, along with the FHC Choir of the Memorial Baptist Mission, took part in the Aomori city-wide crusade at the city auditorium on April 8, 1963. On that occasion, Johnny also served as an interpreter.

Also, Miyoko Asano, another faithful member of the Memorial Baptist Mission and past interpreter for Clyde Wilton, indicated that she participated in the Japan New Life Movement held in Akita, Japan, beginning April 7, 1963. In Akita, she helped translate for Dr. James Parker, and when the crusade finished there on April 14, she helped in the Misawa crusade. A future goal for Miyoko was to study English and the Bible and to become an organist. In a letter as of June 11, 1963, Miyoko indicated that the Augustus Ramsey family and the Thomas

Miyoko Asano

Chevallier family had left Japan for the US mainland by that time. She indicated by photographs sent that Kenichi Yoshida, another faithful member of the mission, was still involved in the Mission work and that the FHC Choir was doing well.

Beginning on April 14, 1963, the Memorial Baptist Mission took part in the Japan New Life Movement held in Misawa City, Japan. The mission sponsored the Texas Mission Team consisting of Marvel Upton from Sunray, Texas, Clarence Boyle from Harlingen, Texas, and Gene Combs from Midland, Texas. Johnny was instrumental in coordinating the crusade, which was the culmination of many hours of prayer and tireless effort. The program consisted of a number of venues in the area and lasted thru April 20, 1963.

The FHC Choir from the mission was featured during the crusade. There were about 159 decisions for Christ during the 7 days of the crusade, and on the last day at the Misawa City Auditorium, Hiroshi Suzuki accepted Christ. As a result of the revival held in Misawa, the membership of the FHC Choir began to rapidly increase. Although the members were not all Christians, the experience was a Christian witness that made changes in some of their lives.

Following the Misawa crusade, Junichi Ishikawa and others were invited to speak on April 22, 1963, at the Misawa Dressmaking School. Although the principal of the school was just interested in cultural knowledge about Christianity as an educational exercise, it was an opportunity to sow the seeds of the Gospel and to let the students know why they needed Christ.

On 1-2 May, 1963, Junichi Ishikawa served as translator for the New Life Movement in Same, Japan. Again, the FHC Choir from Memorial Baptist Mission also attended the crusade to help with the program.

On another engagement, on June 2, 1962, the FHC Choir was invited to present a musical program at the Evening Interlude Program at the Misawa AB Security Wing Chapel. Junichi Ishikawa was the organizer of the presentation. There were separate parts of the program in English and in Japanese. The English portion was directed by SSgt. Willie Barfield, and the Japanese portion was directed by Morio Nokura, a music teacher at the Misawa Senior High School.

Other areas having become aware of the inspirational music of the FHC Choir in the Misawa area, the FHC Choir was invited to participate in the Kitakami Music Crusade held on June 22, 1963. Missionary Holecek and his congregation were hoping to start the same kind of program in the city of Kitakami, Japan. The city was located about 123 miles south of Misawa in the Iwate Prefecture. The crusade at Kitakami was successful, having more than 350 in attendance.

At this time the FHC Choir had 22 members, and the choir stayed in Kitakami overnight to participate the next day, Sunday, at the morning service conducted by Bro. Holecek. Also a member of the choir, Yoshio Kabutoya helped in the Sunday School, with the FHC Choir singing for the children. Missionary Holecek was favorably impressed by Yoshio's skillful way of responding to the children and the conducting of the Sunday School. Willie Barefield was also present with the choir and helped in the regular service with his talent in singing.

Willie Barefield

After moving to Texas in July 1962, Clyde Wilton accepted a position in January 1963 as the pastor of the Trimmier Road Baptist Chapel (later renamed the Skyline Baptist Church) in Killeen, Texas. Even though he was half a world away from Japan, he still kept ties with Memorial Baptist Mission members. Beginning in August 1963, Clyde was privileged to sponsor Junichi Ishikawa for a two-month preaching and witnessing crusade in the USA. At that time Johnny was still with the Misawa AB Chapel as a language specialist, and he was given leave time to make the trip to America. Arriving first in Los Angeles, California, on August 17, 1963, Johnny met with Glenn Shanahan, a personal friend and colleague of Clyde Wilton, for a week of speaking engagements in California. For part of the time in California he met with his former supervisor at Misawa, Chaplain Frank Griffin, who was then stationed at George AFB, California. Chaplain Griffin arranged for Johnny to speak at one of the base chapels.

Following the time in California, Johnny next spent a week in Killeen, Texas, for a revival at the Trimmier Road Baptist Chapel, where Clyde Wilton was the pastor. After a fellowship supper on August 24, 1963, Johnny preached each night at the chapel through August 30, 1963.

Junichi Ishikawa at Trimmier Road Baptist Chapel, August 1963

After leaving Killen, Texas, on August 31, 1963, Johnny spent 5 days in Corpus Christi, Texas, until September 6, 1963, when he travelled to San Antonio, Texas. He was in San Antonio for several days with Chaplain Henry Pennington, another military acquaintance from Misawa, and he spoke a number of times at the Lackland Baptist Church. Johnny then returned briefly to Killeen, Texas, before travelling to north Texas, where he spoke at Mineral Wells, Dundee, Kamay, Fort Worth, Sunray, and Temple, Texas. Johnny was able to experience a variety of Texas towns, from the small town of Dundee, near where Clyde's brother, Anthony Wilton, lived, to the large city of Fort Worth, where he met with Franklin Jeffus, another friend who was stationed for a while at Misawa AB. While at Sunray, Texas, Johnny met with Marvel Upton, who was one of the preachers that went to Japan for the New Life Crusade in which Johnny was an interpreter.

From Temple, Texas, on September 19, 1963, Johnny travelled to Atlanta, Georgia, where he spent time with Dr. James Wesberry and spoke at the Morningside Baptist Church and the Atlanta Baptist Ministers Conference. Johnny had met Dr. Wesberry when he came to Misawa AB for a Protestant Preaching Mission in October 1960 and to meet with the Misawa Baptist Mission.

After leaving Georgia on September 24, 1963, Johnny spent some time in North Carolina visiting with Chaplain Joseph Coggins, one of the Baptist chaplains who was formerly at Misawa AB. Then, beginning on September 29, 1963, he spent time in Florida with MSgt. James Kelley, who was a former member of the Baptist Fellowship at Misawa. On October 10, 1963, Johnny made a flight back to Los Angeles, California, and on the next day he boarded a flight for the return to Japan. Johnny was back to work at Misawa AB, Japan, on October 14, 1963.

After returning to the mainland USA, Clyde was privileged to have a number of colleagues from his days at Misawa AB to come visit and renew old friendships. One of the first to come to his new home in Killeen, Texas, was Doug Hanna. While at Misawa AB beginning in 1960, Doug was a faithful participant in the activities of the Baptist Fellowship, and he was a member of the VAN Club. Being a new Christian at the time, Doug considered Clyde his mentor and "anchor" for his Christian walk, and he spent time each week with the Wilton family. On his return from Misawa, Japan, in December 1962, Doug was stationed at Sherman, Texas, which was about 220 miles away from Killeen, Texas. After leaving the military service in December 1963, Doug worked as a computer technician for about 15 years, and then he became an employment recruitment agent.

Doug Hanna

Another faithful participant with the Misawa Baptist Mission and the Baptist Fellowship while stationed at Misawa AB in 1960, who came to visit Clyde Wilton in Killeen, Texas, was Clayton

Clayton Spohn

Spohn. He and a number of other airmen had been regular guests in the Wilton home at Misawa AB.

There were a number of other faithful contributors to the life of the Misawa Baptist Mission who had a longtime correspondence with Clyde Wilton but did not make the trip to Texas for a visit. One of those correspondents was Harry Mann. Although of the Methodist denomination, Harry was a positive influence in attending both the mission and the Baptist Worship. After leaving Misawa, Harry became a Methodist pastor in Florida. While living in Florida, he obtained a Doctor of Ministry Degree from the Columbia Theological Seminary near Atlanta, Georgia.

Harry Mann

Space does not permit including all those who were positive influences for the Misawa Baptist Mission, but at least one more bears mentioning. His name was Charles Smith, and he too participated at the mission and the Baptist Worship services at Misawa AB. Charles was also a Methodist, but that did not deter him from being associated with the Baptist Fellowship.

Charles Smith

As membership began to grow at the Memorial Baptist Mission, primarily from its English-speaking members, it became expedient for the congregation to split into two groups. Beginning June 10, 1964, a thirteen member group from the mission, after they had already met and prayed for a new church, made a decision to organize into a new church body. On July 11, 1964, the group undertook sponsorship of the Memorial Baptist Mission; and on July 19, 1964, the English-speaking members of the mission formally organized themselves into the Calvary Baptist Church of Misawa, while the Japanese members remained as the Memorial Baptist Mission. This step was a fulfillment of one of the original goals of the mission to form a Baptist mission that was for and run by Japanese people. Much of the conducting of worship services and administrative planning was already done by them, and now the future of the mission was more in their hands. The Calvary Baptist Church continued to support the mission until it finally became the self-supporting and fully autonomous Misawa Baptist Church in 1988.

About September 1964, there was another member of the Memorial Baptist Mission, Yoshio Kabutoya, who was in communication with Clyde Wilton in Killeen, Texas, and wanting to come to the USA for study. Clyde was able to sponsor Yoshio, who had been a dedicated member of the mission for a number of years. On September 6, 1964, Yoshio preached a sermon at the evening worship at Skyline Baptist Church, where Clyde was the pastor, and soon afterward he began attending Mary Hardin-Baylor College in Belton, Texas, which was about 17 miles away from Killeen. It was Yoshio's goal to study to work in full-time Christian ministry. Mary Hardin-Baylor College was a women's school, where men were allowed to attend but not graduate. After finishing a course of study at the college, they would be expected to transfer to another school for graduation. Yoshio studied for about three years at Mary Hardin-Baylor before returning to Japan in July 1967.

Yoshio Kabutoya

On January 31, 1965, while Yoshio Kabutoya was still in Killeen, Texas, Joseph Coggins came to Killeen for a visit with Clyde Wilton and family. Joseph Coggins was another Baptist chaplain who served at the

From Left: Clyde Wilton, Joseph Coggins, Yoshio Kabutoya.

Misawa AB Chapel with Clyde. All three were involved in the ministry of the Memorial Baptist Mission.

Another renewed friendship with a colleague from Misawa AB occurred in June 1965, when Clyde Wilton agreed to conduct a week of revival with Eli Wiltshire of the Travilah Baptist Church in Travilah, Maryland. While in Misawa, Eli had worked with the Baptist Fellowship, where he was in charge of the Friday Evening Prayer Meeting, a member of the Baptist Fellowship Committee, and he preached on occasion at the Baptist Worship Service at the base chapel. Beginning on June 20, 1965, Clyde preached daily thru June 27, 1965, at the Travilah Baptist Church where Eli was the pastor.

Eli Wiltshire

In May 1967, another member at the Memorial Baptist Mission, Hiroshi Suzuki, sought to study in the USA under the sponsorship of Clyde Wilton. Hiroshi had graduated with a BA Degree in English in Japan, and he was then pursuing a MA Degree in English. It was Hiroshi's ambition at that time to become a writer. On May 17, 1967, Hiroshi arrived in California from Japan. On May 21, 1967, he arrived in Killeen, Texas, and on May 28, 1967, he preached a sermon at the evening worship service at Skyline Baptist Church in Killeen. After visiting for a while with the Wilton family, Hiroshi left Killeen on August 31, 1967, to attend school at Howard Payne College in Brownwood, Texas.

Hiroshi Suzuki

Hiroshi continued in school at Howard Payne College until the summer of 1970. Then, beginning in the fall of 1970, he attended the Golden Gate Baptist Theological Seminary in Valley Mill, California, where he was a student until the spring of 1973. In May 1973, Hiroshi moved to New York where he worked for a while for the Home Mission Board as an English Instructor. He eventually made his home in New York where he worked as a Christian counselor.

On July 22, 1967, Yoshio Kabutoya returned to Japan from his studies in Texas. Junichi Ishikawa met him at the Tokyo International Airport. After meeting the Japan Baptist Convention staff, Yoshio was expecting to attend the annual Baptist Pastor's Conference at Amagi on August 4-7, 1967, after which Yoshio would become the pastor for the Memorial Baptist Mission. It was Johnny's joy that Yoshio would be a spiritual leader for the mission, and he was planning to have him as the main speaker in 1967 Baptist revival meetings at the Misawa, Yokawame, and Tsubo missions. At that time, the Memorial Baptist Mission was supporting missions at Yokawame and Tsubo.

Johnny reported that there were then enthusiastic and hard-working members at the Memorial Baptist Mission. Four members were sent to the Baptist Youth Fellowship Conference at Amagi in June 1967, and plans were to send three high school students to attend the Baptist Japan-Wide Student Conference at Amagi in July 1967. There was also the possibility of starting a new mission work at Sanbongi City, Japan (near Towada). In addition, on July 19, 1967, the mission planned to sponsor an evening concert at the civic center (Misawa). Johnny would be speaking at the Tohoku Gakuin University Glee Club Concert at the civic center.

In August 1969, Clyde Wilton participated in the India New Life Crusade in Ajmer, India. On the trip to India, he stopped over for one night in Tokyo, Japan, arriving on August 5, 1969. While he was in Tokyo, Clyde was able to meet briefly with Yoshio Kabutoya and Miyoko Asano. Miyoko was then attending school at the Seinan Gakuin Seminary in Fukuoka, Japan, located on the southern island of Kyushu.

*Tokyo, Japan, 5 Aug 1969;
From Left: Yoshio Kabutoya,
Miyoko Asano.*

In December 1969, there was a Christmas party at the Memorial Baptist Mission, where Yoshio Kabuotya was still in leadership. The mission still supported the Tsubo Mission and the Yokawame Mission, with sponsorship from the Calvary Baptist Church. According to the major events published by the Calvary Baptist Church, mission work had begun at Tsubo in June 1964, but mission work was later discontinued in September 1983.

CHAPTER 4

MISAWA BAPTIST CHURCH

After the English-speaking Calvary Baptist Church was separated from the Memorial Baptist Mission in July 19, 1964, the Calvary Baptist Church became the sponsor for the mission. It was later on October 14, 1981, that the Calvary Baptist Church agreed to supply needed funds to help the mission call a regular pastor. However, as the mission moved toward becoming self-supporting, they requested in May 7, 1986, that the financial assistance from the Calvary Baptist Church be reduced. Then, on September 1988, the mission became organized as a fully autonomous, self-supporting church of the Japan Baptist Convention. It was then that the name of the mission was changed to the Misawa Baptist Church, and the pastor was at that time Shunro Sakamoto.

Through the years, Clyde Wilton continued to correspond with friends of the Misawa Baptist Church, and in 1991, he was invited to meet in Japan with Johnny Ishikawa. Accompanied with his daughter, Fawncyne Wilton, Clyde made a ten-day trip to Japan beginning on May 30, 1991. After leaving Houston, Texas, and passing through Los Angeles, California, they arrived in Tokyo, Japan, on May 31, 1991.

Johnny was then living with his family in Tokyo. He had left Misawa a number of years previously becoming a Christian businessman. For 14 years he worked with HomCare Ltd. as one of the foundation members. Then he established a marketing company named the ConCorde

Corporation. Although no longer associated with the Misawa Baptist Mission, Johnny was active with the Camp Zama Baptist Church, located about 25 miles southwest of Tokyo.

Camp Zama Baptist Church, Japan, 2 June 1991; From Left: Junichi Ishikawa, Mr. & Mrs. Amano, Fawncyne Wilton.

While in Tokyo, Clyde met again with Miyoko Asano, who was then working with the Japanese Baptist Convention in Tokyo. Then, on June 7, 1991, Clyde went for a side trip to Misawa, Japan, stopping first in Hachinohe to meet with Yoshio Katuboya, who had been working for an educational supply company and had been helping at the Hachinohe Baptist Church. Yoshio accompanied Clyde to Misawa, where Clyde visited Misawa Baptist Church and areas of Misawa AB where he once lived.

From Left: Yoshio Kabutoya, Clyde Wilton....

Misawa Baptist Church, 7 June 1991; From Left: Yoshio Kabutoya, Clyde Wilton.

Calvary Baptist Church, 7 June 1991, Clyde Wilton

As of June 1991, Shunro Sakamoto, who was the first pastor at the Misawa Baptist Church after it became self-supporting, was no longer the pastor. Instead, Mr. Iwase, a lay preacher, was filling in at the church. On Sunday, June 9, 1991, Clyde and Fawncyne attended the Sunday morning Sunday School and Worship Service. On this day the Lord's Supper was observed.

Misawa Baptist Church, 9 June 1991, Clyde Wilton

Misawa Baptist Church, 9 June 1991, Clyde Wilton (center)

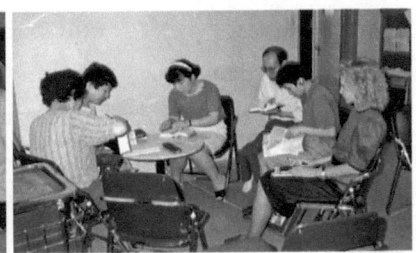
Misawa Baptist Church, 9 June 1991, Fawncyne Wilton (right)

MEMORIES OF THE MISAWA BAPTIST MISSION

Misawa Baptist Church,
9 June 1991

Misawa Baptist Church,
9 June 1991

On June 9, 1991, Clyde had a last look at the train station in Misawa before boarding for the trip to Tokyo. Then, on June 10, 1991, Clyde & Fawncyne said their final good-bye to Japan as they left Tokyo for home in Texas.

Misawa train station,
9 June 1991, Clyde Wilton

Tokyo International Airport,
10 June 1991,
Fawncyne Wilton

In April 1999, Clyde had another opportunity to meet with a friend from Misawa, Japan. Ronald Williams, who worked with the early Misawa Baptist Mission and had become a leader in the Foursquare Church after leaving the military, came for a visit with Clyde while on a church assignment in Texas. At that time, Ron was the Chief Communications Officer of the Foursquare Church with headquarters in California, and he had come to Dallas, Texas, to coordinate a conference being held there. Ron took a side trip from Dallas to be with the Wilton family in Bryan, Texas, on April 11, 1999.

Emmanuel Baptist Church, Bryan, Texas, 11 Apr 1999; From Left: Clyde Wilton, Larue Wilton (seated), Carolyn Williams, Ron Williams.

Having witnessed the Baptist mission at Misawa from its birth to its maturity, Clyde could say that he had been truly blessed of the Lord for the opportunity to play a part in the ministry of the Misawa Baptist Mission/Church. Over the years that followed, he continued to communicate with friends he had made while associated with the mission work, but now more from a distance. However, as always he prayed for the work and did everything he could to do his part to spread the Gospel message as exemplified by the dedicated work at Misawa.

PICTURE CREDITS

MEMORIES OF THE MISAWA BAPTIST MISSION

Page	Subject
Front Cover	Memorial Baptist Mission, Misawa City, Japan, c. 13 Oct 1961 (Wilton family photograph).
x	From map of the Japan Chugoku Region large highlighted (Public Domain).
1	Clyde Wilton in uniform at Misawa AB, Japan, c. 1 Jan 1960 (Wilton family photograph).
2	Construction of the Wilton home at D-306, B-Battery, Misawa City, Japan, c. 13 July 1959 (Wilton family photograph).
2	Clyde Wilton at Wilton home after completion at D-306, B-Battery, Misawa City, Japan, c. 22 July 1959 (Wilton family photograph).
3	Calvin Doyle at Wilton home at D-306 in B-Battery, Misawa City, Japan, 13 October 1959 (Wilton family photograph).
4	TSgt. Robert Nickell at bathhouse baptism in Misawa City, Japan, 16 Oct 1959 (Wilton family photograph; Public Domain).
5	Alfred Martin at home in B-Battery, Misawa City, Japan, c. 13 October 1961 (Wilton family photograph).
5	MSgt. George Ashcraft at bathhouse baptism in Misawa City, Japan, 16 Oct 1959 (Wilton family photograph; Public Domain).
6	Hiroshi Minokawa & harmonica at Memorial Baptist Mission, Misawa City, Japan, c. 25 Dec 1961 (Wilton family photograph).
6	Joseph Coggins at Misawa AB Chapel, Japan, 22 Nov 1960 (Wilton family photograph).
6	Ronald Williams, Wilton residence at 202C, Misawa AB, Japan, c. 19 August 1961 (Wilton family photograph).

PICTURE CREDITS

Page	Subject
7	Junichi Ishikawa/bathhouse baptism, Misawa, Japan, 16 Oct 1959 (Wilton family photograph).
7	VAN Club gathering at Furumaki Train Station near Misawa, Japan, c. 3 October 1959 (Wilton family photograph).
7	Rice field in Aomori Prefecture, Japan, c. 3 Oct 1959 (Wilton family photograph).
7	VAN Club gathering at Shingo/Herai Village, Amori Prefecture, Japan, c. 3 Oct 1959 (Wilton family photograph).
8	Clyde Wilton and John Andre playing checkers on VAN Club picnic at Shingo/Herai Village near Aomori, Japan, c. 3 October 1959 (Wilton family photograph).
8	First rented building of the Baptist Fellowship for Christian worship services in Misawa City, Japan, Feb 1961 (Wilton family photograph).
9	Bathhouse baptism in Misawa City, Japan, 16 Oct 1959 (Wilton family slide).
10	Baptist doctrinal class in the Wilton home at D-306 in B-Battery, Misawa City, Japan, c. 21 Nov 1959 (Wilton family photograph).
11	Milton DuPriest at Misawa City, Japan, Feb 1961 (Wilton family photograph).
13	Misawa Baptist Mission rented building on B-Battery Road, Misawa City, Japan, c. May 1961 (Wilton family slide).
13	Sign in front of Misawa Baptist Mission on B-Battery Road, Misawa City, Japan, c. 10 Sept 1960 (Wilton family photograph).

Page	Subject
14	Joseph Coggins preaching at Misawa Baptist Mission Dedication Ceremony, B-Battery Road, Misawa City, Japan, 3 Feb 1960 (Wilton family photograph; Public Domain).
14	Clyde Wilton teaching at the Misawa Baptist Mission, B-Battery Road, Misawa City, Japan, c. 13 Aug 1960 (Wilton family photograph).
15	Missionaries Halverson and Heiss with wives at Misawa AB Chapel, c. 10 Dec 1959 (Wilton family photograph).
15	Hannah Barlow at Hakodate City Overlook, Hakodate, Japan, c. 10 June 1960 (Wilton family photograph).
15	James Kelley at the Misawa AB Chapel Men's Work Day, c. 18 March 1961 (Wilton family photograph).
16	Akita Baptist Church of Akita, Japan, 13 May 1962 (Wilton family photograph).
16	Toyohara Sensei and wife at Wilton home E-19 at Misawa AB, Japan, 2 April 1960 (Wilton family photograph).
16	Missionary Hannah Barlow visiting at Wilton home E-19 at Misawa AB, Japan, with Baptist Fellowship social, 14 May 1960 (Wilton family photograph).
17	Thomasine Allen visiting at the Wilton home at E-19 Misawa AB, Japan, 5 Aug 1960 (Wilton family photograph).
18	Front of Misawa Baptist Mission on B-Battery Road during revival, c. 22 July 1960 (Wilton family photograph).
18	Japanese men at VAN Club picnic at Lake Ogawara, Japan, 23 July 1960 (Wilton family photograph).
18	VAN Club picnic at Lake Ogawara, Japan, 23 July 1960 (Wilton family photograph).

PICTURE CREDITS

Page	Subject
19	Baptism for new member Kenichi Yoshida at Lake Ogawara, Japan, 29 Oct 1960 (Wilton family photograph).
19	Baptism for new member Kenichi Yoshida at Lake Ogawara, Japan, 29 Oct 1960 (Wilton family photograph).
19	Dr. James Wesberry in front of Misawa Baptist Mission on B-Battery Road, c. 17 October 1960 (Wilton family photograph).
19	Departure of Bob Keith from the dependents airport terminal at Misawa AB, Japan, c. 1 Feb 1961 (Wilton family photograph).
20	Financial goal chart during fund meeting at Misawa Baptist Mission on B-Battery Road, Feb 1961 (Wilton family photograph).
21	Coleman Clarke and group viewing land for the Memorial Baptist Mission, Misawa, Japan, c. 28 Apr 1961 (Wilton family photograph).
21	Misawa Baptist Mission group during final negotiations with Aiba Construction for the new Memorial Baptist Mission building, c. 10 July 1961 (Wilton family photograph).
22	Baptist Worship service at Misawa AB Chapel, Japan, 21 Apr 1961 (Wilton family photo).
22	Baptist group at Kawashima sisters baptism at Misawa City bathhouse, Misawa, Japan, 22 Apr 1961 (Wilton family photograph).
22	Clyde Wilton/Kawashima sisters after baptism at Misawa City bathhouse, Japan, 22 Apr 1961 (Wilton family photograph).
23	Tokichi Konno speaking at Memorial Baptist Mission Groundbreaking Ceremony, Misawa City, Japan, 4 June 1961 (Wilton family photo).

Page	Subject
23	Joseph Coggins praying at Memorial Baptist Mission Groundbreaking Ceremony, Misawa City, Japan, 4 June 1961 (Wilton family photo).
23	Japanese Baptist mission members at Memorial Baptist Mission Groundbreaking Ceremony, Misawa City, Japan, 4 June 1961 (Wilton family photograph).
24	Coggins Sayonara Party, Misawa AB, Japan, c. 12 June 1961 (Wilton family photograph).
24	Baptist Fellowship group at Amagi Baptist Assembly, Japan, 20 June 1961 (Wilton family photograph).
25	Hiroshi Suzuki in front yard/Wilton residence at S-96-C, Misawa AB, Japan, c. 15 July 1961 (Wilton family photograph).
25	Clyde Wilton with Hiroshi Suzuki in Wilton residence S-96-C, Misawa AB, Japan, c. 21 Aug 1961 (Wilton family photograph).
26	Hiroshi Suzuki with chapel staff at Misawa AB Chapel, Japan, c. 4 August 1961 (Wilton family photograph).
27	Ronald Williams at Sayonara Party at Wilton residence S-96-C, Misawa AB, Japan, c. 19 Aug 1961 (Wilton family photograph).
28	Foundation preparation at building site for the Memorial Baptist Mission, Misawa City, Japan, c. 15 July 1961 (Wilton family photograph).
28	Foundation construction at building site for the Memorial Baptist Mission, Misawa City, Japan, c. 22 July 1961 (Wilton family photo).
28	Baptistery construction inside the Memorial Baptist Mission building, Misawa City, Japan, c. 10 Aug 1961 (Wilton family photograph).

PICTURE CREDITS

Page	Subject
28	Steeple & entry construction at the Memorial Baptist Mission building, Misawa City, Japan, c. 23 Aug 1961 (Wilton family photograph).
28	Sign removal from old Misawa Baptist Mission site on B-Battery Road, Misawa City, Japan, c. 29 Sept 1961 (Wilton family photograph).
28	Front entrance to Memorial Baptist Mission, Misawa City, Japan, after construction done, c. 29 Sept 1961 (Wilton family photograph).
29	Baptist Fellowship mission trip to leper colony near Aomori, Japan, c, 16 Sept 1961 (Wilton family photograph).
31	Tokichi Konno giving Call To Worship at the Dedication Service for the Memorial Baptist Mission, Misawa City, Japan, 6 October 1961 (Wilton family photograph).
32	Milton DuPriest bringing the message at the Dedication Service for the Memorial Baptist Mission, Misawa City, Japan, 6 October 1961 (Wilton family photograph).
32	Augustus Ramsey giving the Report at the Dedication Service for the Memorial Baptist Mission, Misawa City, Japan, 6 October 1961 (Wilton family photograph).
32	Clyde Wilton at the Dedication Service for the Memorial Baptist Mission, Misawa City, Japan, 6 Oct 1961 (Wilton family photograph).
32	Japanese members at the Dedication Service for the Memorial Baptist Mission, Misawa City, Japan, 6 Oct 1961 (Wilton family photograph).
33	Borror family/Misawa AB Passenger Terminal, Japan, 16 Oct 1961 (Wilton family photograph).
33	Earl Varner & family at Misawa AB Terminal, Japan, c. 20 Nov 1961 (Wilton family photo).

Page	Subject
33	Clyde Wilton baptizing Fawncyne Wilton at the Memorial Baptist Mission, Misawa, Japan, 29 Nov 1961 (Wilton family photograph).
33	Baptism at Memorial Baptist Mission, Misawa City, Japan, 29 Nov 1961 (Wilton family photo).
34	Bonnie Sandberg at VAN Club preparation for yearly Christmas packages, Misawa AB, Japan, c. 16 Dec 1961 (Wilton family photograph).
34	Sayonara gathering for the Sandberg family at the Misawa AB Chapel, Japan, c, 8 Dec 1961 (Wilton family photograph).
34	Aomori Baptist Church Young People in front of Wilton residence S-96-C, Misawa AB, Japan, 12 Jan 1962 (Wilton family photograph).
35	Takeshi Yahabe & Thomasine Allen at Wilton residence S-96-C, Misawa AB, Japan, c. 9 Feb 1962 (Wilton family photograph).
35	Session at the Pastor's Evangelistic Conference at the Memorial Baptist Mission, Misawa City, Japan, c. 15 Feb 1962 (Wilton family photo).
35	Group picture of pastors and attendees at the Pastor's Evangelistic Conference held at the Memorial Baptist Mission, Misawa City, Japan, c. 16 Feb 1962 (Wilton family photograph).
36	Shimizu sensei at Wilton residence at S-96-C, Misawa AB, Japan, 6 Apr 1962 (Wilton family photograph).
36	Shimizu sensei with group at Wilton home at S-96-C, Misawa AB, Japan, 6 Apr 1962, (Wilton family photograph).

PICTURE CREDITS

Page	Subject
36	Japanese members on Easter 1962 at front of Memorial Baptist Mission, Misawa City, Japan, 22 Apr 1962 (Wilton family photograph).
36	Members at Memorial Baptist Mission, Misawa City, Japan, 22 Apr 1962 (Wilton family photo).
37	Sayonara Party for Clyde & Larue Wilton at the Memorial Baptist Mission, Misawa City, Japan, c. 9 June 1962 (Wilton family slide).
38	Thomas Chevallier at Williamson residence at Misawa AB, Japan, c. 6 Jan 1962 (Wilton family photograph).
38	Miyoko Asano at entry to the Memorial Baptist Mission, Misawa City, Japan, c. 15 Nov 1961 (Wilton family photograph).
40	Willie Barefield in special music at the Misawa AB Chapel, Japan, c. 6 Mar 1961 (Wilton family photograph).
41	Junichi Ishikawa by sign at the Trimmier Road Baptist Chapel, Killeen, Texas, c. 9 Sept 1963 (Wilton family photograph).
41	Clyde Wilton/Junichi Ishikawa at the pulpit at Trimmier Road Baptist Chapel, Killeen, Texas, c. 9 Sept 1963 (Wilton family photograph).
42	Doug Hanna in front of Wilton home at 618 Bishop Drive, Killeen, Texas, Feb 1965 (Wilton family photo).
42	Clayton Spohn at Wilton home at E-19, Misawa AB, Japan, 25 Dec 1960 (Wilton family photo).
43	Harry Mann at Misawa AB, Japan, c. 31 Mar 1961 (Wilton family photograph).
43	Charles Smith at Wilton home at E-19, Misawa AB, Japan, 25 Dec 1960 (Wilton family photo).

MEMORIES OF THE MISAWA BAPTIST MISSION

Page	Subject
44	Yoshio Kabutoya in yard at the Trimmier Road Baptist Chapel, Killeen, Texas, c 6 September 1964 (Wilton family photograph).
44	Clyde Wilton with Joseph Coggins and Yoshio Kabutoya in front of the Wilton home at 618 Bishop Drive in Killeen, Texas, 31 January 1965 (Wilton family photograph).
45	Eli Wiltsire at the Gunn residence, Misawa AB, Japan, c. 29 Jan 1962 (Wilton family photo).
45	Hiroshi Sizuki standing in yard at the Skyline Baptist Church, Killeen, Texas, c. 28 May 1967 (Wilton family photograph).
47	Yoshio Kabutoya and Miyoko Asano standing in park at Tokyo, Japan, 5 August 1969 (Wilton family photograph).
50	Junichi Ishikawa, the Amanos, and Fawncyne Wilton at entrance to Camp Zama Baptist Church, 2 June 1991 (Wilton family photo).
50	Clyde Wilton & Yoshio Kabutoya at Kabutoya home, Hachinohe, Japan, 7 June 1991 (Wilton family photograph).
51	Yoshio Kabutoya and Clyde Wilton standing in front of Misawa Baptist Church, Misawa City, Japan, 7 June 1991 (Wilton family photograph).
51	Clyde Wilton at the entrance to Calvary Baptist Church, Misawa, Japan, 7 June 1991 (Wilton family photograph).
51	Clyde Wilton at pulpit before worship service at Misawa Baptist Church, Misawa City, Japan, 9 June 1991 (Wilton family photograph).

PICTURE CREDITS

Page	Subject
51	Clyde Wilton standing with Japanese members inside Misawa Baptist Church, Misawa, Japan, 9 June 1991 (Wilton family photograph).
51	Fawncyne Wilton with Sunday School Class at Misawa Baptist Church, Misawa, Japan, 9 June 1991 (Wilton family photograph).
52	Church members at Misawa Baptist Church, Misawa City, Japan, 9 June 1991 (Wilton family photograph).
52	Lord's Supper Service, Misawa Baptist Church, Misawa City, Japan, 9 June 1991 (Wilton family photograph).
52	Clyde Wilton waiting for the train at Misawa Station, Misawa, Japan, 9 June 1991 (Wilton family photograph).
52	Fawncyne Wilton, Tokyo International Airport, Japan, 10 June 1991 (Wilton family photo).
53	Ronald Williams & Clyde Wilton with wives at the Emmanuel Baptist Church in Bryan, Texas, 11 Apr 1999 (Wilton family photograph).
Back Cover	Members planting a cross during the Memorial Baptist Mission Groundbreaking Ceremony at Misawa City, Japan, 4 June 1961 (Wilton family photograph).

INDEX OF NAMES

(By Last Name)

Page	Subject
Adams, Betty Jo	36, 36 (picture), 37 (picture)
Allen, Thomasine	17, 17 (picture), 35, 35 (picture)
Amano, Masaaki	17, 18 (picture), 35 (picture)
Andre, John	7, 8 (picture)
Asano, Miyoko	17, 18, 23 (picture), 32 (picture), 36 (picture), 37 (picture), 38, 38 (picture), 46, 47 (picture), 50
Ashcraft, George	4, 5, 5 (picture), 9 (picture), 10, 11, 13
Barefield, Willie	20, 31, 40, 40 (picture)
Barlow, Hannah	15, 15 (picture), 16, 16 (picture), 22, 22 (picture)
Bateman, Edwin	16, 22 (picture)
Best, Doris	37 (picture)
Best, Roger	37 (picture)
Borror, Bill	24 (picture), 32, 33 (picture)
Borror, Jo Ruth	24 (picture), 33 (picture)
Boyle, Clarence	39
Chevallier, Kitty	37 (picture)
Chevallier, Thomas	21, 21 (picture), 37 (picture), 38, 38 (picture), 39
Childers, Larry	31

Page	Subject
Clarke, Coleman	11, 21, 21 (picture), 24
Coggins, Jean	19 (picture), 24 (picture)
Coggins, Joseph	6, 6 (picture), 13, 14, 14 (picture), 23, 23 (picture), 24, 24 (picture), 42, 44, 44 (picture)
Combs, Gene	39
Cooney, Jerald	26 (picture)
Crums	v (preface)
Davis, Kenneth	5
Dosier, Edwin	5
Doyle, Calvin	viii (preface), 3, 3 (picture), 11, 13
DuPriest, Milton	11, 11 (picture), 20, 31, 32 (picture), 35, 35 (picture), 38
Easters	v (preface)
Fujimoto, Takeyuki	36 (picture), 37 (picture)
Fukuhara, Takeshi	21, 21 (picture)
Gates, Richard	4, 9 (picture)
Griffin, Frank	26 (picture), 41
Gunn, Patsy	37 (picture)
Haley, Larue V.	vi (preface)
Halverson, Carl	15, 15 (picture)
Hanna, Doug	34 (picture), 42, 42 (picture)
Hedler, Paul	21 (picture), 24 (picture)
Heiss, Donald	8, 11, 15, 15 (picture), 24, 24 (picture), 34, 34 (picture), 35 (picture)
Heiss, Joyce	15 (picture), 24 (picture)
Holecek, Missionary (Frank)	40
Hotai, Ken	34, 34 (picture), 35 (picture)
Hubers	v (preface)

INDEX OF NAMES

Page	Subject
Ishikawa, Junichi	1, 7, 7 (picture), 9, 9 (picture), 10 (picture), 14, 14 (picture), 18, 20, 23, 23 (picture), 26, 29, 31, 32 (picture), 35 (picture), 36 (picture), 37 (picture), 37, 38, 39, 40, 41, 41 (picture), 42, 46, 49, 50, 50 (picture), Back Cover
Ishikawa, Setsuko	37 (picture)
Iwase, Mr.	51
Jeffus, Franklin	4, 9 (picture), 41
Johnson, L.C.	36, 36 (picture)
Jones, Fumiko	18
Kabutoya, Yoshio	36 (picture), 37 (picture), 40, 44, 44 (picture), 46, 47, 47 (picture), 50, 50 (picture), 51 (picture)
Kawashima, Mutsu	22, 22 (picture), 23 (pictures), 32 (picture), 36 (picture), 37 (picture),
Kawashima, Saki	22, 22 (picture), 23 (picture), 36 (picture), 37 (picture)
Keith, Bob	19, 19 (picture), 20
Kelley, James	13, 15, 15 (picture), 17, 19 (picture), 20, 20 (picture), 21 (picture), 23 (picture), 31, 42
Kinnards	v (preface)
Konno, Taheshi	18
Konno, Tokichi	10 (picture), 18, 18 (picture), 21, 21 (picture), 23 (pictures), 31, 31 (picture), 36 (picture), 37 (picture), Back Cover
Madison, Marshall	18
Mann, Harry	34 (picture), 43, 43 (picture)

Page	Subject
Martin, Alfred Ronald	18
Martin, Alfred Ulman	5, 5 (picture), 6, 8, 9 (picture), 13, 31
Meade, John	36, 36 (picture)
Meade, Linda	33 (picture)
Minokawa, Hiroshi	6, 6 (picture), 9, 9 (picture), 10 (picture), 13, 18, 37 (picture)
Nickell, Robert	4, 4 (picture), 9 (picture)
Nokura, Morio	40
Ohnuma, Tadashi	6, 18 (picture)
Parker, James	38
Pennington, Henry	41
Ramsey, Augustus	31, 32 (picture), 38
Ramsey, Ruby	34 (picture)
Ray, Kay	33 (picture)
Rhodes, Woodie	31
Sakamoto, Shunro	49, 51
Sandberg, Bonnie	34, 34 (picture)
Sandberg, Ronald	34 (picture)
Sandberg, Sheri	34 (picture)
Seward, Mrs.	33 (picture)
Seward, Tommy	33 (picture)
Shanahan, Glen	40
Shimizu, Mr.	36, 36 (picture)
Skaggs, Franklin	13, 14 (picture)
Smith, Charles	43, 43 (picture)
Spohn, Clayton	42-43, 42 (picture)
Straus, Kimie	18, 22 (picture)
Suzuki, Hiroshi	24-26, 25 (pictures), 26 (picture), 39, 45-46, 45 (picture)
Tonosaki, Taeko	18, 23 (picture), 31, 36 (picture), 37 (picture)

INDEX OF NAMES

Page	Subject
Toyoharas	16, 16 (picture)
Underwood, George	35 (picture)
Upton, Marvel	39, 41
Varner, Beverly	24 (picture), 33 (picture)
Varner, Brenda	33 (picture)
Varner, Earl	8 (picture), 20, 20 (picture), 21 (pictures), 24 (picture), 31, 32, 33 (picture)
Varner, Mrs. Earl	24 (picture), 33 (picture)
Varner, Ronald	24 (picture), 33 (picture)
Wasberry, James	19, 19 (picture), 41-42
Webb, Mr.	34 (picture)
Williams, Carolyn	53 (picture)
Williams, Ronald	6, 6 (picture), 15, 22 (picture), 23, 23 (picture), 26-27, 27 (picture), 52, 53 (picture)
Wilton, Aaron	24 (picture)
Wilton, Charles Anthony	v (preface), 41
Wilton, Clyde	1 (picture), 2 (picture), 8 (picture), 10 (picture), 13 (picture), 14 (picture), 16 (picture), 19 (picture), 22 (picture), 24 (picture), 25 (picture), 32 (picture), 33 (picture), 37 (picture), 41 (picture), 44 (picture), 50 (picture), 51 (pictures), 52 (picture), 53 (picture)
Wilton, Elmer E. & Eula	v (preface)
Wilton, Fawncyne	33 (picture), 49, 50 (picture), 51, 51 (picture), 52, 52 (picture)
Wilton, Kathy	24 (picture), 33 (picture)
Wilton, Larue	vi-vii, 9 (picture), 20, 24 (picture), 37 (picture), 53 (picture)

Page	Subject
Wilton, Luther V.	v (preface)
Wilton, Stanley	9 (picture), 13 (picture), 24 (picture)
Wiltshire, Eli	34 (picture), 37 (picture), 45, 45 (picture)
Yahabe, Takeshi	35, 35 (picture)
Yamagishi, Mamoru	9, 9 (picture), 18 (picture), 22
Yamamura, Yukiko	36 (picture), 37 (picture)
Yokayama, Mr.	23 (picture), 32 (picture)
Yoshida, Kenichi	18, 19 (picture), 23 (picture), 32 (picture), 36 (picture), 37 (picture), 39, Back Cover

www.ingramcontent.com/pod-product-compliance
Lightning Source LLC
LaVergne TN
LVHW042247070526
838201LV00089B/63